Countries of the World

Panama

by Marc Tyler Nobleman

Bridgestone Books

an imprint of Capstone Press
Mankato, Minnesota

Bridgestone Books are published by Capstone Press
151 Good Counsel Drive, P.O. Box 669, Mankato, Minnesota 56002
http://www.capstone-press.com

Library of Congress Cataloging-in-Publication Data
Nobleman, Marc Tyler.
    Panama/by Marc Tyler Nobleman.
    p. cm.—(Countries of the world)
Includes bibliographical references and index.
    ISBN 0-7368-1372-1 (hardcover)
    1. Panama—Juvenile literature. I. Title. II. Countries of the world (Mankato, Minn.)
F1563.2 .N63 2003
972.87—dc21   2001008082

Summary: Introduces the geography, animals, food, and culture of Panama.

Editorial Credits
Christopher Harbo, editor; Karen Risch, product planning editor; Patrick Dentinger, book
    designer and illustrator; Alta Schaffer, photo researcher

Photo Credits
Capstone Press/Gary Sundermeyer, 5 (bottom) *Coins courtesy of Rachel Caven*
CORBIS/Paul Almasy, 12; Reuter/Alberto Lowe, 14; Paul A. Souders, 18
Cory Langley, cover
Dave G. Houser/Houserstock, 10
Joe Viesti/The Viesti Collection, Inc., 20
Robert Caputo/Aurora, 16
Stockhaus Limited, 5 (top)
Woodfin Camp and Associates, Inc./Robert Frerck, 6, 8

**Bridgestone Books thanks Juan Carlos Galeano, Ph.D., Director of Latin American and
Caribbean Studies at Florida State University, for his help in reviewing this book.**

1 2 3 4 5 6 07 06 05 04 03 02

Table of Contents

Fast Facts. 4
Maps 4
Flag 5
Currency 5

The Land 7
Cities. 9
The People 11
Going to School 13
Panamanian Food 15
Animals 17
Sports and Music. 19
Holidays and Celebrations 21

Hands On: ¡Usted es el Mono! 22
Learn to Speak Spanish. 23
Words to Know 23
Read More 24
Useful Addresses and Internet Sites 24
Index. 24

Fast Facts

Name: Republic of Panama

Capital: Panama City

Population: Almost 3 million

Main Languages: Spanish (official), English

Religions: Roman Catholic, Protestant

Size: 30,193 square miles
(78,200 square kilometers)
Panama is slightly smaller than the U.S. state of South Carolina.

Crops: Bananas, rice, sugarcane, coffee, corn

Maps

Flag

Panama's flag is blue, red, and white. Blue stands for the Conservative political party in Panama. Red represents the Liberal political party. White is a symbol of peace. The flag has two stars. The blue star stands for honesty. The red star represents law.

Currency

The unit of currency in Panama is the balboa. One hundred centesimos equal one balboa. Panama uses the U.S. dollar as well as the balboa.

In the early 2000s, 1 balboa equaled 1 U.S. dollar. About .6 balboa equaled 1 Canadian dollar.

The Land

Panama is a country in Central America. Colombia lies to the east of Panama. Costa Rica borders Panama to the west. The Caribbean Sea is on the northern coast of Panama. The Pacific Ocean borders the southern coast. Most of Panama has a tropical climate. The weather is warm and wet.

Panama is narrow. It connects North America and South America. The narrowest part of Panama is only 30 miles (48 kilometers) wide.

The Panama Canal cuts through Panama. This waterway was built in 1914. The canal connects the Pacific and Atlantic Oceans. Ships travel through the Panama Canal. They do not need to make the long trip around South America.

Panama has mountains and rain forests. The Tabasara Mountains rise in the west. The San Blas Mountains and Darien Mountains rise in the east. Rain forests also stand in eastern Panama.

Tugboats help large ships travel through the Panama Canal.

Cities

The capital of Panama is Panama City. It is Panama's largest city. More than 700,000 people live there.

Panama City is on the Pacific coast. It is east of the Panama Canal. In the 1500s, Spanish settlers moved to Panama. They built beautiful buildings in Panama City. Some of these buildings still stand. Today, the city has many restaurants, museums, and churches.

Colón is another large city in Panama. Colón is on Panama's northern coast, near the Panama Canal. More than 207,000 people live there. Colón has the world's second largest free trade zone. This zone lets companies buy and sell products without paying taxes.

Many products are made in Panama's cities. Some of the products include clothing, chemicals, and cement. Panama also has businesses that sell sugar, bananas, cocoa, and oil.

Panama City has many apartment buildings and churches.

The People

More than half of Panama's population lives in urban areas. The rest live in rural areas. Many Panamanians live near the Panama Canal. Some people work at the canal. Other people work in stores or businesses near the canal.

Most people who do not live near the Panama Canal are farmers. People with small farms grow rice and corn for their families. Some people with large farms grow sugarcane and coffee to sell to other countries.

Native tribes live in Panama's rural areas. These tribes include the Choco (CHO-co), Guaymi (KWA-mee), and Kuna (KOO-na). The Kuna sometimes are called San Blas Indians. The tribes have lived in Panama for hundreds of years. Natives farm and fish to make a living.

Spanish is the official language of Panama. Some people speak English. Many Panamanians wear the same style of clothes as North Americans.

Kuna women make colorful fabrics called molas.

Going to School

People in Panama care about education. The government spends a lot of money to improve education. Elementary school is free. The school year lasts from April to December. Students learn reading, writing, and math. They also learn about history and art.

Children from age 6 to 15 must go to school. A law says they must complete sixth grade. Some families pay for children to go to private middle school and high school. Many students attend colleges in Panama City.

Middle school and high school are called secondary education in Panama. Students study many subjects in the first three years. They learn math, science, art, and history. The second part of secondary education also lasts three years. Students study only one subject in the second part. They choose a subject that will help them get a job after they graduate.

Panamanian children gather outside a school in Panama City.

These women are making rice for a large group of people.

Panamanian Food

People eat rice with almost every meal in Panama. Beans and corn also are common foods. Guacho (GWA-cho) is rice soup with beans. Bollo (BOH-yo) is a boiled corn dish. Tortillas (tor-TEE-yas) also are popular in Panama. People make these flat breads from corn or wheat.

Sancocho (sahn-KOH-cho) is Panama's national dish. A national dish is the official food of a country. People make this stew with spicy vegetables and chicken.

Panamanians eat a lot of meat and seafood. Guisado (kwee-SA-doh) is a stew with meat and tomatoes. Panamanians sometimes add fish to soup.

Panamanian families usually eat together. They have a big breakfast. The main meal with rice, meat, and vegetables is in the middle of the day. Families often eat a small meal in the evening.

Animals

Many wild animals live in Panama. Monkeys climb in the trees. Jaguars roam in the rain forests. Panama also has anteaters, armadillos, and sloths.

Capybaras (kap-uh-BAHR-uhs) live in Panama. Panamanian capybaras weigh about 60 pounds (27 kilograms). They eat plants. They live in forests and on grasslands. Capybaras also spend a lot of time in water to keep cool.

Many fish and animals swim in the oceans near Panama. One type of fish is called an anchoveta (an-cho-VAY-ta). Another fish is herring. Anchoveta and herring swim in the Gulf of Panama. Giant sea turtles lay eggs on Panama's beaches.

Panama's national parks have many birds. People visit parks to see eagles, parrots, parakeets, and toucans. Quetzals (ket-SALS) also live in Panama. These colorful birds have long tail feathers.

The capybara is the largest rodent in the world.

Sports and Music

Baseball is the most popular sport in Panama. Many Americans moved to Panama to work after the canal opened in 1914. Panamanians learned how to play baseball from these Americans.

Water sports also are popular in Panama. People like to snorkel and scuba dive. Snorkeling is swimming underwater near the surface. Scuba diving is swimming far below the water's surface. Snorkelers and scuba divers use equipment so they can breathe underwater.

Panamanians enjoy many other sports. People in Panama like to play basketball. Their national basketball team plays in other countries. People also enjoy soccer, boxing, cycling, and tennis.

People in Panama enjoy music and dancing. Many Panamanians go to music concerts. Some people play musical instruments such as guitars and accordions. Panamanians often dance at festivals and celebrations.

Panamanian children play Little League baseball.

Holidays and Celebrations

Panamanians celebrate many holidays and fiestas (fee-ESS-tuhs). A fiesta is a festival. Some people dress in traditional clothes on holidays and at fiestas. Women wear a pollera (po-YER-a). This costume includes a colorful shirt and a wide skirt. Men wear a montuno (mon-TU-noh). A montuno is a white shirt and short pants.

Panamanians celebrate Independence Day on November 3. Panama became independent from Colombia on this date in 1903. People have parades and watch fireworks on Independence Day.

Carnival is a big party in Panama. People sing and dance in the streets. They wear masks and costumes. Carnival is in February or March. It lasts four days.

People celebrate Christmas in Panama on December 25. They decorate their homes. They eat large meals and exchange gifts on Christmas Day.

Panamanian women decorate their hair with jewelry when they wear polleras.

Hands On: ¡Usted es el Mono!

Panamanian children often play this game to practice their counting skills.

What You Need

Two or more players

What You Do

1. One player picks a number between 0 and 9. The player says the number out loud. The player says, "Whoever says this number is the monkey!"
2. The players take turns counting in order. Each player says one number at a time.
3. The players must skip any number that has the chosen number. If the chosen number is 4, they must skip 4, 14, 24, 34, 40, and so on.
4. A player who forgets to skip the chosen number is out. When a player says the chosen number, the other players say, "¡Usted es el Mono!" This means, "You are the monkey," in Spanish.
5. The player who is the monkey begins the game again by picking a new number.

Learn to Speak Spanish

hello	hola	(OH-lah)
good-bye	adiós	(ah-dee-OHSS)
please	por favor	(POR fah-VOR)
thank you	gracias	(GRAH-see-as)
yes	sí	(SEE)
no	no	(NOH)
good morning	buenos días	(BWAY-nohs DEE-ahs)
good night	buenas noches	(BWAY-nahs NOH-chehs)
excuse me	discúlpeme	(dees-KOOL-peh-may)

Words to Know

accordion (uh-KOR-dee-uhn)—a musical instrument that players squeeze to make sound; accordions have keys and buttons.

costume (KOSS-toom)—clothes worn by people during a traditional celebration or holiday

rodent (ROHD-uhnt)—a small mammal with long, front teeth used for gnawing; mice and rats are rodents.

rural (RUR-uhl)—away from cities and towns

scuba (SKOO-buh)—self-contained underwater breathing apparatus; divers use scuba equipment to breathe underwater.

snorkeling (SNOR-kuhl-ing)—underwater swimming while breathing through a tube

Read More

Park, Ted. *Taking Your Camera to Panama.* Austin, Texas: Steadwell Books, 2001.

Rau, Dana Meachen. *Panama.* A True Book. New York: Children's Press, 1999.

Useful Addresses and Internet Sites

Embassy of Panama in Canada
130 Albert Street
Suite 300
Ottawa, ON K1P 5G4
Canada

Embassy of Panama in the United States
2862 McGill Terrace NW
Washington, DC 20008

Panama National Parks
http://www.panamatours.com/Rainforest/Rainforest_intro.htm
The World Factbook—Panama
http://www.cia.gov/cia/publications/factbook/geos/pm.html

Index

anchoveta, 17
baseball, 19
capybaras, 17
Carnival, 21
Colón, 9

fiesta, 21
food, 15
mountains, 7
natives, 11
Panama Canal, 7, 9, 11

Panama City, 9, 13
pollera, 21
quetzals, 17
rain forests, 7, 17
school, 13